Sketchbook
Composition Studies for Film

Hans P Bacher

Sketchbook
Composition Studies for Film

Laurence King Publishing, London

A TALISMAN BOOK FOR LAURENCE KING

First published in 2015
Second impression in 2019
Third impression in 2023

Talisman Publishing Pte Ltd
talisman@apdsing.com
www.talismanpublishing.com

Laurence King Publishing Ltd
Carmelite House,
50 Victoria Embankment,
Temple, London EC4Y 0DZ, UK
robert.wiltshire@hachette.co.uk

A catalogue record for this book is available from the British Library

ISBN 978-178-06-7596-1

Printed in Singapore

introduction

The first time I started to realize how important a good composition is was during the style-development for Disney's *Mulan*. Before I had done more or less intuitive compositions, but had not really followed rules or analyzed how other artists had come up with their solutions.

Through studying Asian art I learned how important it is to balance all the elements in your image, the *yin* and *yang* in composition – big/small, dark/bright, straight/curved, heavy/light, busy/peaceful and so on.

And I analyzed the right placement of characters in an environment, the different ways to create depth, the triangle rule for more than two characters in a composition, the changing point-of-views (or camera angles) and, especially for storyboarding, the best combination of just the right images, the editing and rhythm of close-ups and wide shots.

The first studies came from the Masters in Art, and further from breaking down hundreds of live action films into their specific Visual Language, in several thousand thumbnails and sketches.

For this sketchbook I selected a few to give you some ideas for compositions, show you the wide variety of staging and creating the most interesting shots. It is a work in progress – I am still learning, and having fun...

If you are making a nature documentary movie you shoot what you can get. During a typhoon disaster you are not necessarily looking for the best camera angles.

But in a live action or animated feature film *you* decide about every single shot, nothing is accidental. Usually every single scene is carefully planned in a storyboard, the best possible rhythm of a sequence has to be worked out. Especially in animation the shot order and layout in the so-called *workbook*, a more defined next step after the storyboard, is already the edited version of the final film. In live action films, most important in special effects and action sequences, a precise planned storyboard saves the producer a lot of time and money.

I don't want to go too much into detail in this book – it is just a 'sketchbook' – but I will give you a few ideas about some basic rules in film-making defining the composition in every single shot.

establishing
in wideshots

emotion
in close ups

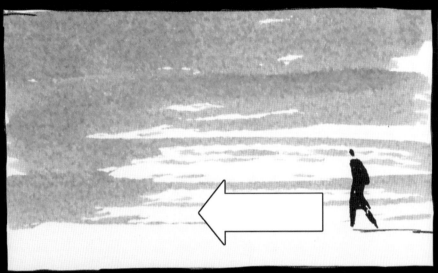

direction
in movement

perspective
into the picture

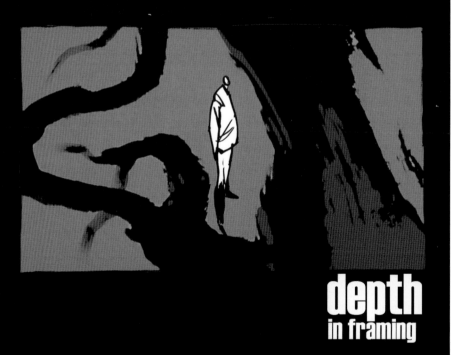

depth
in framing

**with emphasis on
submission or dominance**

downshot

dark in front of light
light in front of dark

single character

Choreography

This combined movement of camera and actors in one scene has to be planned extremely carefully. It is comparable to the movement of dancers in a ballet on stage. The Italian director Michelangelo Antonioni was a master of this kind of *mise en scène*. All movements have to be planned in a floorplan, the same way the ballet-choreographer works. According to the action and dialogue between several involved actors in a scene, the position of the actors is constantly changing. The camera has to follow these changes and has to find an interesting composition for every single key-pose. These key-poses are not accidental, they follow the interaction and the camera can either follow them, or lead their movement in advance. During such a longer scene the compositions in camera can change from extreme close-ups to medium- and long-shots, as well as cover a changing number of actors.

mass-scene

simplicity

You have to reduce all different elements in the frame to a few simple shapes. Overloading the frame with too much detail means the eye doesn't know where to look. There is no need to define every rock and blade of grass especially in the background — just an overall impression of the scene is much better.

Same goes with ideas. Don't try to put too many ideas into a single image. This makes the composition muddy and confusing. Not a good strategy for film where the audience only has a few seconds to interpret each shot. Say one thing with one shot and use a different shot to say something else.

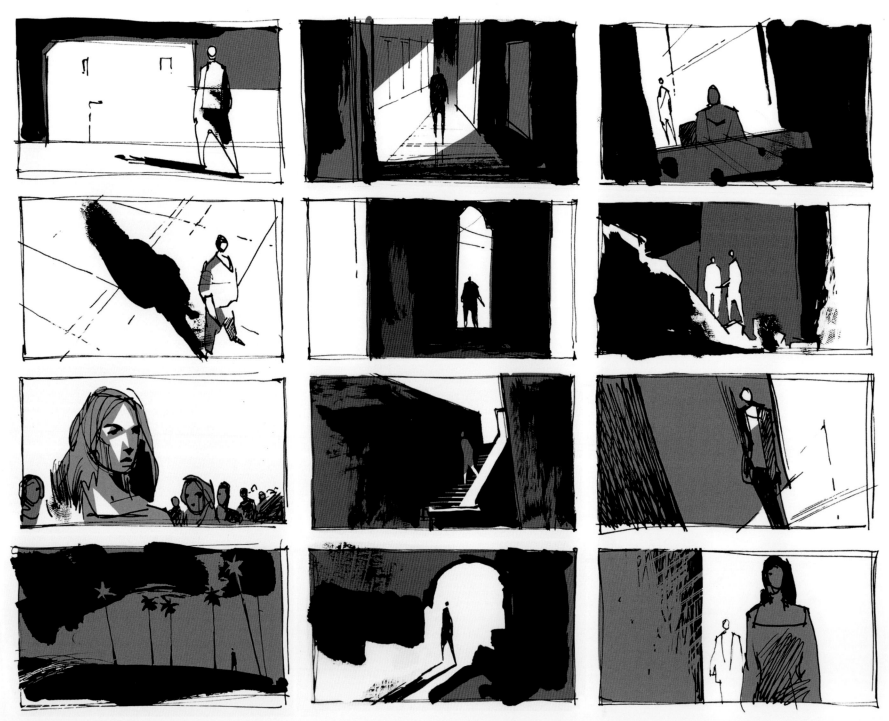

rules

Rules about composition such as the golden section or rule of thirds can certainly help you create good images. But don't think that this is the only way. Once you have understood and practiced the basic rules for quite some time, you should not let these limit you.

Some of the most interesting and important cinema was made because someone decided to break a rule and try something new. Of course you cannot just come in and decide to start breaking the rules before you even know what they are. You need to know what you are doing first and there is a lot which the masters of film over time have learnt that you can use to make your own images and films better. But who knows, perhaps you will eventually break some rule which everyone told you not to break and come up with something completely new and incredible. That might suddenly become the new rule.

chaos

The recent fashion in CG heavy films of covering every square inch of the frame with lots of detail, constantly moving the camera and then adding lots of lens flares and light blooms on top of everything else should be avoided. The goal there seems to be merely to stimulate when instead it should be to communicate. There is a big difference between the two.

Throwing everything and the kitchen sink into the frame in an attempt to hold the audience's attention seems to assume we are making films for chimpanzees. Such compositions are far too chaotic to allow for any kind of bold statement. Making carefully thought out choices, requires more thought and effort, but results in incredible images. And much better ways of stimulating the audience too.

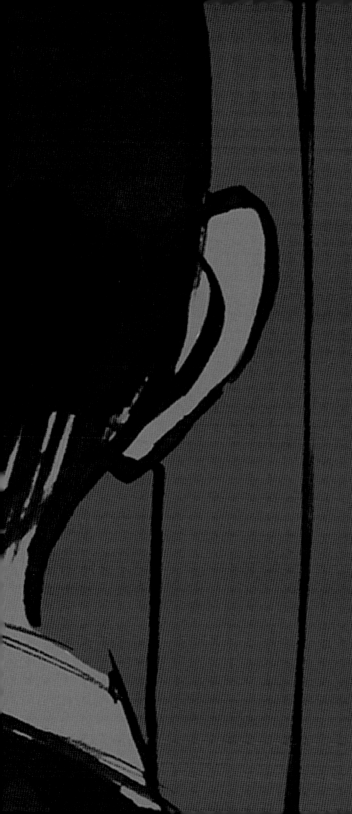

harmony

What we perceive as beauty in images is often a harmonious arrangement of the elements within the frame. A large part of this is about finding the right balance between opposing elements in the composition. Positive and Negative space, detail and no detail, colour and desaturated areas. Each of these have to have both opposites present in the frame in order to work. Some will be more dominant than the other, and this will help give the composition a focal point as well as unify it, but it takes both sides of the coin in the frame for it to work.

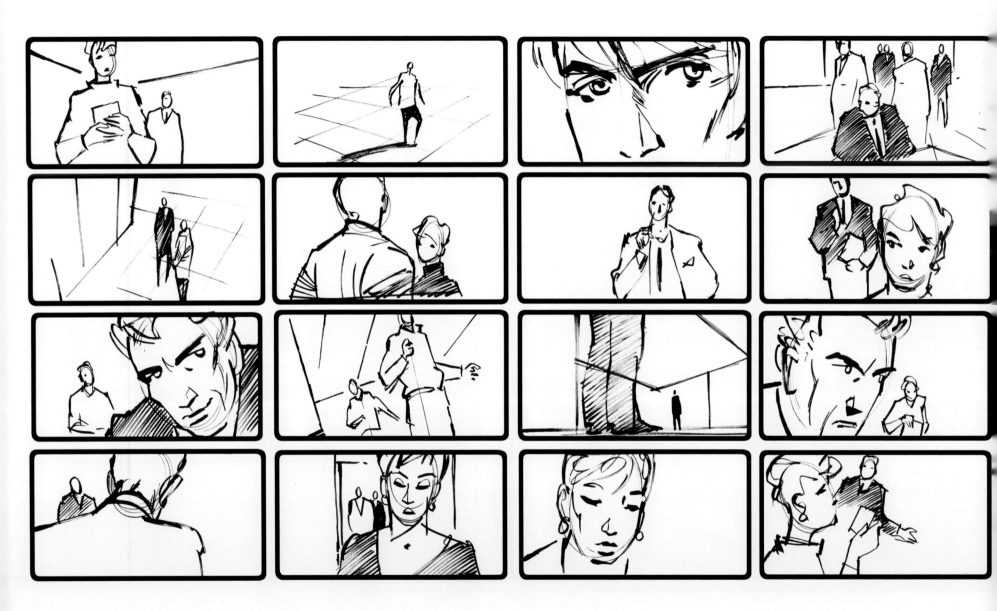

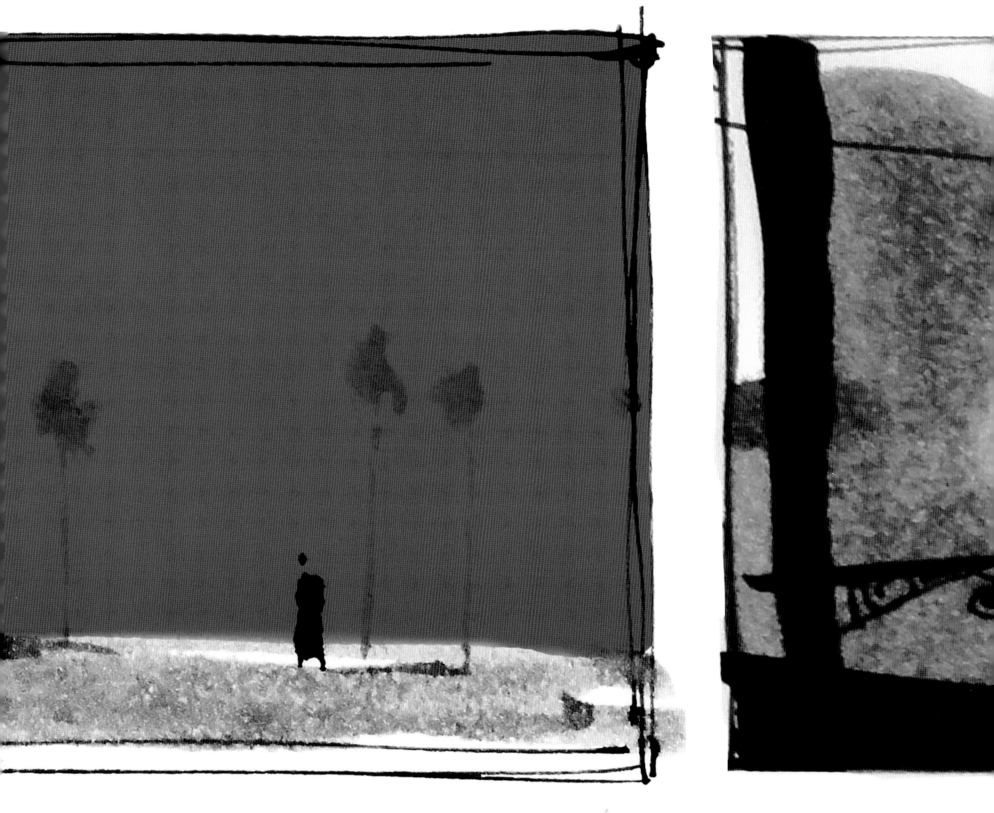

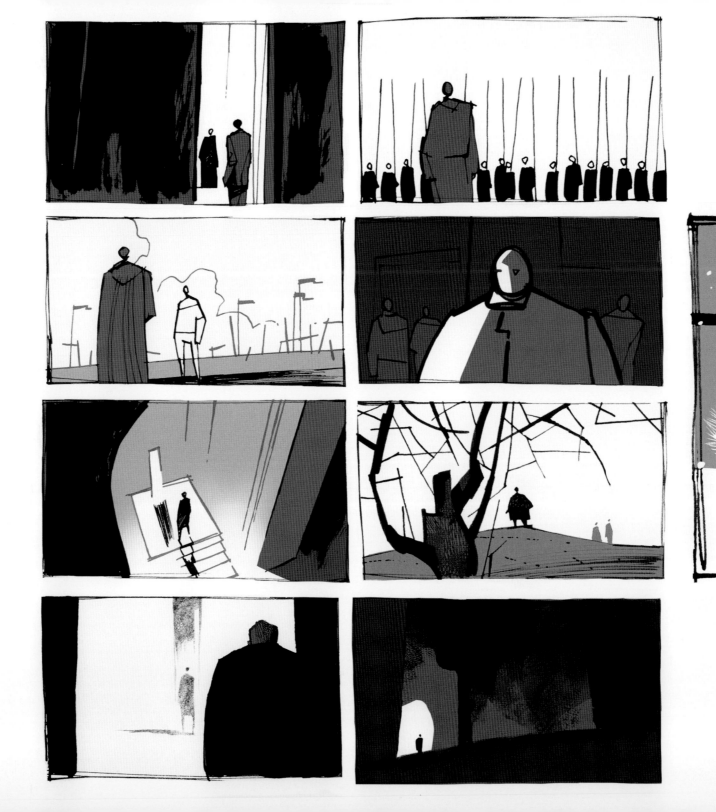

Acknowledgements

Over the past 60-plus years, I have had several advisers, teachers and good friends who have helped me to find my way through a lot of chaos to where I am today.

I would like to thank them – my parents and my late wife Hanne, Hans Flauaus, Guenter Reker, Otto Naescher, Paul Schuellner, Willy Fleckhaus, Andreas Deja, Harald Siepermann, Richard Williams, Uli Meyer, Werner Kubny, Don Hahn, John Watkiss, Mike Smith, Simon Wells, June Foray, Bill+Fini Littlejohn, Tom Schumacher, Joe Grant, Daan Jippes, Barry Cook, Peter Schneider, Umesh Shukla, Tom Sito, Alex Nino, Chen-Yi Chang, Rosemarie Soriaga, Imee Marcos, Marge Randolph, Ishu Patel, Kenny Tai, Monte James, Regis Loisel, and Sanatan Suryavanshi.